D0712756

COMMON-SENSE ENGLISH GRAMMAR

# Common-Sense English Grammar

## Clarabelle D. Decker

*Former Elementary and Secondary School
and University Teacher and Librarian,
Former School Library Supervisor
of Clark County, Nevada*

EXPOSITION PRESS    SMITHTOWN, NEW YORK

FIRST EDITION

LIBRARY OF CONGRESS CATALOG CARD NUMBER: 80-65127

ISBN 0-682-49578-6

Printed in the United States of America

To my English teachers at Northern Arizona Normal School and Northern Arizona State Teachers' College (both now Northern Arizona University), the University of Arizona, and to the many students to whom I taught English in the Las Vegas, Nevada, schools

# Contents

# Introduction

The author believes that good grammar is essential in getting and keeping many available jobs in our society; that clarity in writing and speaking is important; that good usage can and should be taught all through the schools. Much of the grammar is logical and can be learned with ease when it is taught by a good teacher. This book is an attempt to show how verbal skills and grammar can be learned in an effective and common-sense manner.

The sentences in this book which are shown as incorrect in the use of English were taken from newspapers and television programs. The people whose sentences are quoted do not understand the rudiments of good grammar and do not have a clear understanding of the importance of writing and speaking correctly.

Every student, in fact, every person should have a good dictionary, one that shows the derivation, the diacritical markings and division of words, the part of speech, the principal parts of verbs, has a biographical section, a gazetteer, list of abbreviations, list of colleges and universities, and other information. *Webster's Collegiate Dictionary,* based on the second or third edition of the unabridged *Webster's Dictionary,* published by G. and C. Merriam Company, is good. The author prefers the fifth edition of the *Collegiate Dictionary,* based on the second edition of the unabridged *Webster's,* but there are other good abridged dictionaries. One should be a frequent user.

# Parts of Speech

It is important to know the parts of speech, because knowing them and how they are used aids in the ability to speak and write correctly.

## NOUNS

A noun is the name of a person, place or thing.
EXAMPLES: boy, city, towel.
There are singular and plural nouns.
EXAMPLES: boy, boys; city, cities; towel, towels.
Nouns are proper and common.
EXAMPLES: John Brown (proper), boy (common).
Common nouns may be concrete or abstract. *Boy* is concrete.
*Kindness, love* are abstract.
If a group is meant (family), the noun is said to be collective.
A noun is used as the subject of a sentence or clause, the object of a verb or of a preposition. Sometimes a noun is used as an adjective (a *dirt* road) and sometimes as an adverb. (He ran *home*.)

1

A noun can show possession (*John's* jacket), indirect address (*Amy,* come here) or be in apposition with another noun. (That is Mary, our *maid.*)


## PRONOUNS


A pronoun takes the place of a noun.

EXAMPLES: I, he, it, she, they, who, me, him, her, them, we, us, whom.

Pronouns as well as nouns can be singular and plural. This is called *number.* They can show possession. If a *noun* ends in "s" the apostrophe showing ownership goes after the "s", but pronouns do not need apostrophes to show ownership.

Examples of possessive pronouns: hers, theirs, ours, its.

When an apostrophe is in the word *its,* it means *it is.*

There are *interrogative* pronouns: which, what, who, etc.

Some pronouns are called *personal:* he, you, she, me, etc.

There are *relative* pronouns: that, who, which, etc. They introduce modifying clauses. (This is the boy *who* went.)

Some pronouns are called *demonstrative* (this, these, those, etc.).

Some are called *indefinite* (few, all, each, etc.).

Some are *reflexive* (myself, himself, yourself, etc.) Reflexive pronouns are not used as subjects.

RIGHT: I did it *myself.*

WRONG: *Yourself* and friend are invited.

RIGHT: *You* and friend are invited.

There are *subject* pronouns and *object* pronouns. Some *subject* pronouns are I, he, she, we, they, who. The *object* pronouns which are most often misused are me, him, her, us, them and whom. If *me* is correct in a sentence, any object pronoun can be used.

EXAMPLE: *Whom* did you see? You did see *me, him, her, them, us, whom.*

Subject pronouns are used as the *subject* of a sentence or

clause. (See definition of a clause.) They are also used after linking (auxiliary) verbs which link the subject and that predicate word.

EXAMPLES: *It* is *I. It could*n't *have been she.* This *boy* is *he* whom I saw.

## AGREEMENT OF PRONOUNS WITH THEIR ANTECEDENTS IN PERSON, NUMBER, GENDER

(*Antecedent*: A noun or word used as a noun to which a pronoun refers.)

RIGHT: A *person* is more likely to survive if *he/she* drives defensively. (*Person* is singular and is the antecedent—goes before, stands for—*he/she,* also singular.)

WRONG: *Everyone* can choose *their* own gift.

RIGHT: *Everyone* can choose *his/her* own gift. (*Everyone* is singular.)

WRONG: You can get poison ivy by touching *someone* who has it on *them* or on *their* clothing.

RIGHT: You can get poison ivy by touching *someone* who has it on *him/her* or on *his/her* clothing.

WRONG: I doubt if *anyone* will have to clean out *their* desk and leave.

RIGHT: I doubt if *anyone* will have to clean out *his/her* desk and leave.

WRONG: When something happens to a *person, they* don't feel it until it is over. (Instead of *they,* the pronoun should be *he* or *she* to agree with *person,* which is singular.)

WRONG: *Everyone* is paying *their* own way. (*Everyone* is singular. The pronoun should be *his* or *her.*)

RIGHT: *No one* knows in what direction *he/she* will travel.

WRONG: *No one* knows in what direction *they* will travel.

WRONG: No judge has the right to tell a *reporter* whether *they* are in pursuit of a story or not.

RIGHT: No judge has the right to tell a *reporter* whether *he/she* is in pursuit of a story or not.

*VERBS*

A verb shows action or state of being. EXAMPLES: The boy *ran*. It *was* a pleasant day.

Linking (auxiliary or helping) verbs such as *is, am, are, was, were, be, been* are important in correct usage because they link the subject to a word in the predicate. If the word in the predicate is a pronoun, it must be a subject pronoun (I, he, she, we, they, who). EXAMPLES: It *was I*. It couldn't *have been she*.

Object pronouns are objects of other verbs (not linking verbs) or objects of prepositions. (See definition of prepositions.) Examples of pronouns used as objects of verbs: Mother *took her* and *me* to the show. She *joined them* and *us*.

Verbs are *transitive* when they have objects. EXAMPLE: The two preceding sentences.

*Intransitive* verbs do not have objects (receiver of the act). EXAMPLE: The apple *was eaten*.

Verbs have what is called *voice*. *Active voice* shows the subject as the actor. (*We saw* Joseph.) *Passive voice* shows that the subject was acted upon. (*Joseph was seen* by us.)

Verbs also have what is called *mode*. *Indicative mode* affirms or denies. (She *went* away. He *did* not *stay*.) *Imperative mode* shows a command. (*Come* here. *Let* me *go*.) *Subjective mode* shows a wish or condition. (I wish I *were* older. If he *were* here you would not go.)

Verbs have *tense*. Tense shows the time of action. The tenses are present tense (I *see* you), past tense (Yesterday I *saw* you), future tense (I *shall see* you), perfect tense (I *have seen* the article), past perfect tense (I *had read* the article), future perfect tense (By next year I *shall have read* many books.) Past perfect tense is used when a sentence in the past tense is interrupted for reference to a preceding occurrence. EXAMPLE: WRONG: My brother had pictures of fish which he caught. RIGHT: My brother had pictures of fish which he *had* caught.

The tense to be used in dependent clauses and infinitives depends upon the time expressed in the principal verb.

WRONG: I intended to have been there.

RIGHT: I intended to be there.

WRONG: We wished you would have come over.

RIGHT: We wished that you would come over.

If the subjunctive is true in the past and present, the present tense is used. EXAMPLE: He told me that Mars *is* (not *was*) closer to the earth.

Verbs are called *regular* and *irregular*. Regular verbs form the past and past participle by adding *ed* (look, looked, looked). Irregular verbs are different in form for the present, past and past participle and are more apt to be misused (see, saw, seen; sing, sang, sung).

Phrases made up of verbs, such as *am going, can do, will be seen,* etc., are called verb phrases.

A verb agrees with the *subject,* even though a plural noun may be in between the verb and subject.

WRONG: The *size* of his shoes *vary.*

RIGHT: The *size* of his shoes *varies.*

If a subject is singular it takes a singular verb even if the singular subjects are joined by *nor* or *or.*

WRONG: Either the *first* or *second* of the runners *were* tall.

RIGHT: Either the *first* or *second* of the runners *was* tall.

Of course if a subject consists of two or more nouns it must have a plural verb. RIGHT: *Riding* and *sleighing are* good sports.

A verb does not agree with the predicate noun; it agrees with the *subject.* WRONG: The worst *part* of the play *were* the comedians. RIGHT: The worst *part* of the play *was* the comedians. RIGHT: The *comedians were* the worst part of the play.

When a sentence begins with *there are* or *there is,* the verb should agree with the noun that follows. WRONG: *There is* excellent *reasons* for what you have done. RIGHT: *There are* excellent *reasons* for what you have done.

## PRINCIPAL PARTS OF VERBS

One should memorize the principal parts of difficult verbs (present, past, past participle), but when in doubt consult the dictionary. To remember the principal parts, say for the present tense, "Today I _____"; for the past tense say, "Yesterday I _____"; for the past participle say, "I have _____." The past participle always has a helping verb (auxiliary), *have, had,* or some form of the verb *to be* (been). We have noted that regular verbs are not difficult, but irregular verbs change the form to change the tense. Some difficult verbs follow.

| *Present* | *Past* | *Past Participle* |
|---|---|---|
| (I) am | (I) was | (I have) been |
| (you) are | (you) were | (you have) been |
| (they) are | (they) were | (they have) been |
| awake | awaked | awaked |
|  | awoke | awoke |
| bear | bore | born |
|  |  | borne |
| begin | began | begun |
| bend | bent | bent |
| bid | bade | bid |
|  | bid | bidden |
| bite | bit | bit |
|  |  | bitten |
| bleed | bled | bled |
| blow | blew | blown |
| break | broke | broken |
| burn | burned | burned |
|  | burnt | burnt |
| burst | burst | burst |
| catch | caught | caught |
| choose | chose | chosen |
| come | came | come |
| deal | dealt | dealt |
| dive | dived | dived |
| do | did | done |
| drag | dragged | dragged |
| draw | drew | drawn |
| dream | dreamt | dreamt |
|  | dreamed | dreamed |
| drink | drank | drunk |
| drive | drove | driven |
| drown | drowned | drowned (one syllable) |

| Present | Past | Past Participle |
|---|---|---|
| dwell | dwelled | dwelled |
| | dwelt | dwelt |
| eat | ate | eaten |
| fall | fell | fallen |
| fight | fought | fought |
| flee | fled | fled |
| flow | flowed | flowed |
| fly | flew | flown |
| forget | forgot | forgot |
| | | forgotten |
| forgive | forgave | forgiven |
| freeze | froze | frozen |
| get | got | gotten |
| | | got |
| go | went | gone |
| grow | grew | grown |
| hang | hung | hung   (Yesterday I hung the clothes on the line. They have hung there all day.) |
| hang | hanged | hanged   (They hanged the man. He was hanged.) |
| hold | held | held |
| kneel | knelt | knelt |
| | kneeled | kneeled |
| know | knew | known |
| lay (put) | laid | laid |
| lead | led | led |
| lend | lent | lent |
| lie (to rest) | lay | lain |
| lie (tell a lie) | lied | lied |
| loose | loosed | loosed |
| lose | lost | lost |
| mean | meant | meant |
| pay | paid | paid |
| prove | proved | proved |
| | | proven |
| read | read | read |
| rid | rid | rid |
| ride | rode | ridden |

| Present | Past | Past Participle |
| --- | --- | --- |
| ring | rang | rung |
| rise | rose | risen |
| run | ran | run |
| see | saw | seen |
| set (put) | set | set |
| shake | shook | shaken |
| shine | shone | shone |
| show | showed | shown |
| shrink | shrank | shrunk |
| sing | sang | sung |
| sit (rest, remain) | sat | sat |
| slink | slunk | slunk |
| speak | spoke | spoken |
| spend | spent | spent |
| spit | spit | spit |
| | spat | spat |
| steal | stole | stolen |
| swear | swore | sworn |
| sweep | swept | swept |
| swim | swam | swum |
| take | took | taken |
| tear | tore | torn |
| throw | threw | thrown |
| tread | trod | trodden |
| | | trod |
| wake | waked | waked |
| | woke | |
| wear | wore | worn |
| weave | wove | woven |
| weep | wept | wept |
| write | wrote | written |

WRONG: The tea was *drank* by all.
RIGHT: The tea was *drunk* by all.
WRONG: I haven't ever *went* there.
RIGHT: I haven't ever *gone* there.
WRONG: She has *rode* that horse.
RIGHT: She has *ridden* that horse.

WRONG: The bell has already *rang*.
RIGHT: The bell has already *rung*.
WRONG: I have *set* there before.
RIGHT: I have *sat* there before.
WRONG: He *swum* a mile.
RIGHT: He *swam* a mile.
WRONG: He had *shook* my hand.
RIGHT: He had *shaken* my hand.
WRONG: She *come* home late.
RIGHT: She *came* home late.
WRONG: You *was* correct. (*You,* singular or plural, takes *were.*)
WRONG: The water had *froze*.
RIGHT: The water had *frozen*.

Do not say I, he, she, we, they *done* it. Use *did*. *Done* has to have a helping (auxiliary) verb.

Do not use *ate, ran, went, wrote* and other past tense verbs as past participles. Past tense verbs do not have helping verbs.

Do not use *knowed* and *busted* as past tense of *know* and *burst*. There are no such words as *knowed* and *busted*. Do not use *come* as past tense. The past tense of *know* is *knew;* of *burst, burst;* of *come, came.*

## ADJECTIVES

An adjective describes or points out. It modifies a noun or pronoun. EXAMPLES: *This* girl is *pretty*. A *tall* man was seen. He is *handsome*.

*This, that, these* and *those* are sometimes adjectives and sometimes pronouns, depending on their use. If they modify nouns they are adjectives; if they do not modify, they are pronouns. EXAMPLES: *This* is my house. (Pronoun) *This* house is mine. (Adjective)

Adjectives have degrees of comparison. The degrees are

called *positive* (old), *comparative* (older), two things compared, *superlative* (oldest), more than two compared.

WRONG: He is the *smallest* of the two.

RIGHT: He is the *smaller* of the two.

Usually *er* is added to the positive degree to form the comparative, and *est* is added to form the superlative degree, but with words of more than one syllable, the words *more, less, most, least* are added. EXAMPLES: She is *more* beautiful than her sister. She is the *most* beautiful of all. He is *less* brilliant than John. He is the *least* competent of the group.

After a verb that pertains to the senses—sound, taste, smell, feel—use an adjective to denote a quality pertaining to the subject. EXAMPLES: He feels *bad*. (Not badly.) If one feels badly, one's sense of feeling is impaired. *Badly* is an adverb, not an adjective. It smells *bad*.

Don't use *more* with the comparative form or the adjective. WRONG: It is *more* better.


## ADVERBS


An adverb answers the questions how, when, where, to what degree. An adverb modifies a verb, verb phrase, adjective or another adverb. EXAMPLES: He runs *slowly*. (Modifies a verb, answers how.) He can run *fast*. (Modifies a verb phrase, answers how.) She is *very* pretty. (Modifies an adjective, answers how.) He walks *very* rapidly. (Modifies another adverb, answers how.) I shall go *tomorrow*. (Modifies a verb phrase, answers when.) I went *there yesterday*. (*There* modifies the verb and answers where; *yesterday* modifies the verb and answers when.)

Most adverbs are compared like adjectives—positive, comparative and superlative degree—but some are not compared at all, for example, *entirely, fatally*. *More* or *less* goes with the comparative degree, *most* and *least* with the superlative degree.

EXAMPLES: He is *less* noisy than she. He is the *least* talkative of the group. He moves *more* slowly than John. He moves *most* quietly of all.


## PREPOSITIONS

A preposition shows relationship between it and another word or words in the sentence. Prepositions take objects: a noun or pronoun or noun clause. (See definition of a clause.) Some common prepositions are in, on, by, to, from, for, with, of, without. Unless these words are followed by an object they are not prepositions. Sometimes they are adverbs: Come *by* for me. He swung *to* and fro. *For* is a conjunction if it connects two clauses: I came, *for* he asked me to come. *For* is a preposition when it has an object: He came *for* John and me. The preposition *for* has two objects, the noun *John* and the pronoun *me*.

WRONG: The lady talked *with* my brother and *I*.

RIGHT: The lady talked *with* my brother and *me*. (Have you noticed that if any *subject* pronoun is correct in a sentence, any other subject pronoun can be used? The same is true of the object pronouns, me, him, her, them, us, etc. He talked *with* my brother and *me*. (*Him, her, them, us* could be used.)


## CONJUNCTIONS

A conjunction connects words or groups of words. Some conjunctions are *so, as, while, because, or, therefore*. They must connect to be conjunctions.

*Coordinate conjunctions* connect clauses of equal value. Some are *and, furthermore, because, in addition, moreover, but, likewise, for, because, undoubtedly*, etc.

*Correlative conjunctions* are used in pairs, such as *not only, but also, neither  nor, either  or*, etc. If a preposition follows one pair of conjunctions, it should follow the other. EXAMPLE: He was good not only *to his father* but also *to all of his relatives*.

*Subordinate conjunctions* connect clauses which are unequal, for example, adverb clauses introduced by *when, before, while, until, meanwhile, because, as, since, so that, unless, although,* etc., and adjective clauses introduced by *who, which, that, whom,* etc.

EXAMPLES: Please stay *while I go into the house.* (Adverb) This is the man *who was with me.* (Adjective)

## *INTERJECTIONS*

An interjection is a word or group of words which show strong feeling. Oh, I see. What a noise! Ouch! Hurrah! Ah, this is nice. Stop! (Of course *stop* is also a verb, and other parts of speech become interjections if they show strong feeling.)

# More Definitions

*CASE*

*Nominative case* includes subjects and predicate nominatives (words after linking verbs; they link the subject to a word in the predicate). For correct usage one should know the nominative pronouns. (They are listed under the section on pronouns.) Predicate nominatives are the same pronouns as if they were subjects, but they are used after linking (auxiliary) verbs. Common linking verbs are *is, am, are, was, were, be, been,* and verb phrases consisting of these verbs when they link the subject to a predicate nominative. EXAMPLES: *It is I.* It *couldn't be she/I, he, they,* etc.

*Objective case* includes nouns or pronouns used as objects of verbs or prepositions.

RIGHT: We *saw him* and *her* at the show.

WRONG: We saw *he* and his brother at the show.

WRONG: I want you and *I* to go on challenging each other.

RIGHT: I *want* you and *me* to go on challenging each other.

WRONG: He talked *to* my brother and *I.*

RIGHT: He talked *to* my brother and *me.* (*Me* is the object of the preposition *to.* Any other preposition would also have to have an object.) One does not misuse nouns that are objects,

13

but one must know the object pronouns, for they are often mis-used. When one speaks one often misuses *who* and *whom,* but when writing the sound is usually not stilted when using them correctly.

WRONG: *Who* did you play with? (*With* is a preposition and must have an object. *Who* is a subject pronoun.)

RIGHT: *Whom* did you play with? With *whom* did you play?

Some grammarians do not want a sentence to end with a preposition, but *whom did you play with* sounds more natural than *with whom did you play. Whom does he speak for* is correct, but as the headline of a magazine article it is perhaps more unnatural than *Who Does He Speak For?*

The magazine article used this headline. Notice that it also ends in a preposition.

WRONG: Please contact *whomever* is closest to you.

RIGHT: Please contact *whoever* is closest to you.

(The clause, *whoever is closest to you,* is a noun clause, the object of the verb *contact. Whoever* is the subject of the noun clause, *Whomever* is an object and, therefore, in the objective case.)


## POSSESSIVE CASE


A noun or pronoun which shows possession is in the possessive case. EXAMPLES: I have *John's* watch. I read *Dickens'* poems. This is *his. Theirs* is larger.


## CLAUSES


A clause is a part of a sentence that contains a subject and a verb. Clauses are independent (principal) and dependent (sub-ordinate). EXAMPLE: When she came to see me, I was very pleased. *When* introduces the dependent or subordinate clause. Both clauses have a subject and a verb. Clauses are adjective, adverb or noun, depending upon their use in the sentence. The clause beginning with *when* is an adverbial clause because it modifies a verb in the independent clause. This is the girl *whom I saw*. (Adjective clause modifying the noun girl.) I can see *what you did*. (Noun clause object of the verb can see.)

## PHRASES

A phrase is a group of words without a subject and a verb. He ran *like a deer*. (A prepositional phrase used as an adverb, answering the question *how*.) *Glancing up*, he could see the man. (This is a participial phrase because *glancing* is a participle— a verbal which may be adjective or adverb, depending upon its use.) Verbals are sometimes like a noun, for example, in the sentence I enjoy *running, running* is a noun, object of the verb *enjoy*. It is called a *gerund* because a gerund is a verbal ending in *ing*. It really is a special form of an infinitive. (See definition of an infinitive.)

## DECLENSION

The changes in a noun, pronoun or adjective to show person, number or case are called declension.

## ELLIPSIS

An elliptical expression is one that is incomplete, so that words have to be understood to make the meaning complete. EXAMPLE: If possible, come early. (If *it is* possible, *you* come early.)

## GERUNDS

As stated above in the section on phrases, a gerund is a verbal ending in *ing* and used as a noun. EXAMPLE: I do not thank you for *going*.

## INFINITIVES

Infinitives are verbals, many of which are preceded by *to: to go, to do,* etc. They can modify and are used as adjectives or adverbs, depending upon what they modify. Many grammarians have a rule against splitting infinitives, but sometimes a sentence is less awkward if one does split the infinitive. The following were taken from news articles:

I subscribed to your magazine *to* always *have* some of Arizona's beauty close at hand. (*Always to have* would have been stilted and awkward.)

If one is lost in the desert, the best advice is *to,* literally, "*keep* cool."

He is said *to* fully *realize* the consequences of his acts.

We need *to* carefully *watch* that the new curriculum will work.

The preceding sentences sound smooth even though the infinitives are split. Some would also sound good if the infinitives were not split. In writing if you do not feel that you should split an infinitive, do not do so.

## MODIFY

To modify means to limit the quality of. EXAMPLE: She is a *very pretty girl*. (*Pretty* modifies *girl*. *Very* modifies *pretty*.)

# Punctuation

There are reasons for punctuation—a pause, to use force—but one should not be indiscriminate in the use of commas, dashes and other punctuation. Know what the reason is for each punctuation mark used.

## CAPITAL LETTERS

Begin a sentence with a capital letter.

Begin the first word of a direct quotation with a capital. EXAMPLE: He said, "*You* must go there."

Usually each first line of a stanza of poetry is capitalized, but not all poetry is so written.

Proper nouns are capitalized. Important words used as proper nouns are also capitalized. EXAMPLES: Mr. Jones is the principal of Rancho High School; This is the Fourth of July; the Catholic Church; the Colosseum; the Democratic Party; Lord Townsend; the Bible; God, Christ; the days of the week; months of the year; the House of Representatives; Senator Hatch; places of business; names of rivers, mountains, states, countries, cities, etc.; North, East, South and West when they are sections of country, not if they denote direction.

17

Adjectives that mean a race or a language should begin with a capital. EXAMPLES: An Asian dance, Indian language, British Museum.

In a title of a book one should capitalize the first word and other important words. One does not capitalize *a, an, and,* or any prepositions that are in the title after the first word. The pronoun *I* is always capitalized, as is the interjection *O.* Abbreviations of proper names are capitalized: Dr., Ariz., etc.

## *PERIODS*

Put a period after a complete declarative or imperative sentence.

Use a period after an abbreviation: e.g., Bros., Mr., Mrs. *Miss* does not need a period. When an abbreviation comes at the end of a sentence, one period suffices.

WRONG: It would be interesting to ask some of our friends what they think of the answer? (This is a statement and should be followed by a period.)

Some initials which stand for words are so well known that one does not need to use a period after them. EXAMPLES: UN, NATO, USA, etc. Sometimes capitals *are* used, and periods.

## *COMMAS*

Use a comma after yes and no at the beginning of a sentence, as *Yes,* I saw her.

A comma is used after the complimentary closing of all letters: Respectfully yours, Sincerely, Truly yours, etc.; in dates: I was born November 3, 1939, in Bellevue, Colorado; after a confirmatory question: I think it's warm, don't you? It's a nice day, isn't it?

Use a comma to prevent incorrect reading of a group of words that belong together: After eating, my father usually takes a nap. I came to a fence and the burro stopped, throwing me into a bush.

Use a comma in contrasted elements: This is for me, not Mary.

Words in apposition are set off by commas: That girl is Louise, my chum in grade school. I live in Phoenix, the largest city in Arizona. (One does not use a comma if the apposition is part of a name, such as Alexander the Great.)

Commas are used with dates that explain other dates and geographical names that explain other names: I saw him in Prescott, Arizona, on August 7, 1977.

One punctuates before and after if a parenthetical word or phrase occurs in the middle of a sentence: I saw you, Mary, at our house. I am disturbed, to put it mildly, at your actions.

Words or phrases in a series should be separated by commas: John, Tom and Harry were there. He combed his hair, looked in the mirror, took a drink and left.

Sometimes one uses a comma before *and* to avoid confusion: We ate rolls, biscuits, eggs, and jam. (Perhaps if a comma were not used here, someone might think that the eggs and jam were mixed together.)

Adjectives in a series are also separated by commas unless the last adjective is closely linked with the noun: I saw a tall, dark, short man. She was a small, quiet professional woman. (*Small* and *quiet* are adjectives, and *professional woman* is used as one noun which *small* and *quiet* modify.)

A comma is used after *she said* if the quotation is short: She said, "We're going to go." Sometimes a colon is used after *said* if the quotation is long.

An indirect quotation does not need a comma between the verb and a clause beginning with *that* or *how*.

RIGHT: He told us that we had nothing more left.

WRONG: She showed, how it all happened.

Do not sprinkle commas needlessly.

Use a comma in a series of phrases as well as single words: She dressed well, wore correct styles, and was an interesting speaker.

Use a comma between clauses that are joined by *or, and, but for* or any other coordinating conjunction: She glanced around, but she could see nothing.

Sometimes short clauses which are joined do not need a comma, but if there is a pause, place a comma between the clauses. The comma should be placed *before,* not after, the conjunction.

Adverbial clauses preceding the main clause are usually set off by commas: Although I like him very much, I do not want to ride with him. If the adverbial clause follows the main clause, the comma may be omitted: We saw them come in when we were outside.

If a clause is close to the noun or pronoun that it modifies, no comma is needed: Women *who are fat* should not wear shorts.

Some clauses which are not really so closely connected to the noun modified are set off by commas: Our cat, which had three black and three white kittens, was only three years old.

Phrases are treated in the same way as clauses.

A comma is used when a person is directly addressed or if there is an element of explanation in the sentence: Let me hear from you, Jane. I, for one, do not care for her. She was, to be sure, unwilling.

Some interjections are set off by commas: That city is, oh, years old. Well, I hope you learned a lesson.

Groups of words made up of a noun or pronoun and a participle are set off by commas: The day being sunny, I went for a swim.


*THE SEMICOLON*


Use a semicolon when there is a division in thought, but when each unit of the sentence is a part of the whole. Usually a semicolon is used between coordinate clauses which are not joined by a conjunction. (Sometimes a period is used, thus making two sentences. EXAMPLE: He ran to the horse; he leaped on his back.)

Sometimes if a sentence is long and the coordinate clauses are joined by a conjunction, or if the clauses have commas within themselves, a semicolon is used for clarity: He came, according to his brother, right at sunset; and after having dinner, went straight to bed.

The semicolon is used between coordinate clauses which are joined by conjunctive adverbs, *accordingly, consequently, besides, hence, nevertheless:* We did the dance incorrectly the first time; consequently let's try some other way.

If clauses are short a comma may be used, but if a clause is introduced by *therefore,* it takes a semicolon.


## THE COLON

A colon is used to show a list, a series of statements, sometimes just a word. EXAMPLES: I have read: *Mill on the Floss, Tale of Two Cities* and *Ivanhoe.* One person stands between Carter and another term: Kennedy. The problem crisis: Where will we get the money?

The colon is used after the greeting of a letter: Dear Sir: Dear John: Gentlemen:


## THE DASH

A dash seems a little longer than a comma and is longer than a hyphen in looks. One doesn't use dashes indiscriminately to end a sentence. A dash may be used informally: She came— if you can believe it—without an invitation.

A dash is almost like parentheses or commas: Construction jobs paid for with federal funds—even in part—must pay prevailing wages to workers. This is—or should be—of serious concern to all. But, oh!—it's spending as usual.

## PARENTHESIS MARKS

Parentheses may be used to inclose words not a part of the main thought of the sentence: If he arrives (and I hope he will), we shall have a good time. (Dashes could be used here.)

RIGHT: I earn twenty-five ($25) dollars a week. I earn twenty-five dollars ($25) a week.

RIGHT: She has three things to do:

   (1) Make the beds.
   (2) Wash the dishes.
   (3) Do the laundry.


## QUOTATION MARKS

Use to inclose a direct quotation.

RIGHT: She said, "Please get me an apple."

WRONG: She said, "to get her an apple." (This is an indirect quotation and should not have a comma after *said* and should not be inclosed with quotation marks.)

When a quotation is interrupted by an expression such as *he said,* an extra set of quotation marks is used. This is called a divided quotation. EXAMPLE: "I hope," John said, "that you are right."

A quotation within a quotation should have only single quotation marks: The school-finance expert said, "For years policy-makers have been told, 'more kids cost more money.' Now they're asking, 'Why don't fewer kids cost less money?' "

A single speech of several sentences should have only one set of quotation marks: He said, "I am sorry I cannot tell you about where I went. I promised not to tell."

Quotation marks may be used in formal writing with nick-names, slang and some other words of very common usage: She is really "a rounder." Two-thirds of the voters think that tax-slashing programs are "a lot of talk."

Quotation marks are used with titles of individual short poems, titles of articles, chapters of books, etc.

## THE APOSTROPHE

Use an apostrophe in a noun, singular or plural, to show possession: The boy's gun, boys' clothes, children's toys, Moses' laws (or Moses's laws).

The pronouns *his, hers, its, theirs, yours* do not take apostrophes to show ownership.

RIGHT: It is theirs. Its eyes are blue.

RIGHT: One's shoes should fit. The other's line is caught. He makes his 8's like threes.

RIGHT: The Smiths and the Joneses are present. (Not showing possession.)

RIGHT: The less developed countries (LDC's) are blamed.

WRONG: The stock market hit it's highest peak today.

RIGHT: The stock market hit its highest peak today.

RIGHT: Theirs is larger than ours.

If a noun, singular or plural, ends in *s,* to show ownership put the apostrophe after the *s* unless there is a new syllable in pronunciation. If there is another syllable, one may add *'s*.

WRONG: Dicken's books, Keat's works.

RIGHT: Dickens' books, Keats' works, Mr. Douglas' girl.

RIGHT: The Douglases live by us. The Douglases' cat.

An apostrophe is used if a letter is left out: aren't, can't, haven't, they're, it's (meaning it is), etc.

To form the plural of letters of the alphabet or numbers one may or may not use an apostrophe: He makes his *8's* or *8s* like *2's* or *2s*. Cross your *t's* or *ts*.

## QUESTION MARK AND EXCLAMATION POINT

Put a question mark after a direct question: Where are you going? When?

Do not put a question mark after an indirect question: He asked where I was going. (This is a declarative sentence, not a question.)

A question mark is used within parentheses to show uncertainty: The painter was born in 1600 (?) and died in 1639.

A question mark when used within a sentence should not be followed by a comma, semicolon or period.

RIGHT: "Where shall I go?" he asked.

WRONG: "Where shall I go?," he asked.

An exclamation point is used after a word or words showing strong feeling: Heavens! The sky is really falling! Well! That's what I thought would happen. Oh! I can't go.

## ITALICS

Italics (underlining) are shown in typing thus: I take Newsweek. He read The Alhambra. Do you read the Review-Journal? Bulletins, operas, etc., plays, paintings, sculptures and films are also underlined in typing. One also underlines foreign words which are not Anglicized: ibid., op. cit., sic. One does not underline common abbreviations such as etc., e.g., AM, PM. (Consult your dictionary when in doubt.)

Words, letters and figures in the following examples are underlined: He makes his 8's like 2's. Do not use & for and in formal writing. One does not pronounce the t in often.

Sometimes a writer underlines a word or words for emphasis. This practice should not be overworked. He was kind; he isn't now.

## THE HYPHEN

The hyphen is used in compound words such as father-in-law (plural is fathers-in-law); to join words before a noun and used as a single adjective: It was a good-looking man; in compound numbers from 21-99 (twenty-one, etc.) Fractions such as three-fourths, etc., have hyphens. Prefixes ex, all, self, and the suffix elect have hyphens in such words as ex-Secretary of State, self-made, all-American, President-elect Jones. Prefixes such as *pre, semi, anti, un,* etc., are often followed by a hyphen, but not always. Examples: pre-Pearl Harbor, mini-series, semi-Gothic, anti-American, un-American (but unnatural). Consult your dictionary when in doubt whether or not a word should have a hyphen.

If one spells out a word one uses a hyphen: A C-A-T was on the roof.

A hyphen is used to divide syllables at the end of a line. Use your dictionary if you aren't sure where a word should be divided. The hyphen should be placed at the end of the first line, not at the beginning of the second line.

# More Correct Usage

WRONG: They were asked *who* they were supporting.

RIGHT: They were asked *whom* they were supporting. (They were supporting *whom, me, them, us*—any object pronoun.)

WRONG: She claims *its* clairvoyance that led her to it. (There should be an apostrophe in *its,* because it means *it is* in this sentence.)

WRONG: None of *its* necessarily good for the city.

RIGHT: None of *it's* necessarily good for the city.

RIGHT: *Its* hair is white.

WRONG: Tell it *like* it is.

RIGHT: Tell it *as* it is. (Since *as* connects two clauses it is a conjunction. *Like* is not a conjunction. It is a verb or a preposition. Examples: I *like* you. Like is a verb. She looks *like* me. *Like* is a preposition.)

WRONG: He was moved around pretty *good* by the people.

RIGHT: He was moved around pretty *well* by the people. (*Good* is an adjective and cannot modify a verb. *Well* in this sentence is an adverb and modifies the verb.)

WRONG: *Every* since I saw him I knew he would go far.

RIGHT: *Ever* since I saw him I knew he would go far.

WRONG: It was a surprise to my wife and *I*.

RIGHT: It was a surprise to my wife and *me*. (To is a prepo-

26

sition and takes an object. One would not say it was a surprise to *I*.)

WRONG: They looked good to *we* old-fashioned folks.

RIGHT: They looked good to *us* old-fashioned folks. (They looked good to *me, us, them,* etc.)

WRONG: The package is *laying* on the porch.

RIGHT: The package is *lying* on the porch. (*Laying* means putting or placing; *lying* means resting or remaining, whether a person or an object such as a package.)

RIGHT: I was *lying* there.

WRONG: I want to thank *whomever* is responsible.

RIGHT: I want to thank *whoever* is responsible. (*Whoever* is the subject of the noun clause, which is the object of the verbal to thank. Since *whoever* is the subject of the noun clause it must be a subject pronoun. One would not say *me, him, her* is responsible. *Whom* is also an object, as you remember.)

WRONG: The rest of the *Light's* vacation was spent in Ohio.

RIGHT: The rest of the *Lights'* vacation was spent in Ohio.

RIGHT: The Jim Lights are home from vacation. (No apostrophe is needed. The family's surname is Light.)

WRONG: This doesn't mean that Smith or Jones *are* unfeeling.

RIGHT: This doesn't mean that Smith or Jones *is* unfeeling. (If the sentence had *and* before Jones, the verb, of course, would be *are,* which is plural.)

WRONG: He says the checks are for *he* and his wife.

RIGHT: He says the checks are for *him* and his wife. (*For* is a preposition and takes an object. *Him* is an object pronoun; *he* is a subject pronoun.)

WRONG: Your beard just *lays* there. (Lays means *put*.)

RIGHT: Your beard just *lies* there. (*Lies* means *remains*.)

WRONG: Each of the men in the picture *were* present at the site. (Each is singular. The verb should agree with the subject in number. The verb should be *was*.)

WRONG: Neither the sheriff *or* any other officer knows of it. (*Neither* goes with *nor*. *Either* goes with *or*.)

WRONG: Finances should be in *real* good shape. (Say *very,* not real in this sentence. *Real* is an adjective, not an adverb. Adjectives do not modify adjectives. *Good* is an adjective. *Really* and *very* are adverbs and can modify the adjective *good*.)

WRONG: *Myself* and James went.

RIGHT: James and *I* went.

WRONG: If I *was him* I would not go.

RIGHT: If I *were he* I would not go. (I am not he, so the verb should be *were*. The pronoun after a linking verb should be a subject pronoun. *He* is a subject pronoun.)

WRONG: He *sure* works *good*.

RIGHT: He *surely* works *well*. (*Sure* and *good* are adjectives and cannot modify the verb *works*.)

WRONG: *No one* is willing to see *their* name in print at this time.

RIGHT: *No one* is willing to see *his* name in print at this time. (*No one* is singular and is the antecedent of *his* or *her*, also singular.)

WRONG: They did not ask him *whom* he thought were the conspirators. (He thought *who* were the conspirators. The clause has to have a subject. *Whom* is an object.)

WRONG: Good luck to the candidate, *whomever* he may be. (The pronoun should be *whoever*. *Be* is a linking verb and takes a subject pronoun as the predicate nominative.)

WRONG: It took John and *I* three strokes to reach the drive. (The pronoun should be *me*, the object of the verb *took*. One would not say it took *I*—or any other subject pronoun.)

RIGHT: He looks *suspicious*. (*Suspicious* is an adjective after the linking verb *looks*.)

RIGHT: He looked *suspiciously* at the red car. (*Suspiciously* is an adverb and modifies *looked*, which is not a linking verb in this sentence.)

WRONG: People asked me *whom* I thought would be elected.

RIGHT: People asked me *who* I thought would be elected. (I thought *he*—or another subject pronoun—would be elected. *Who* is the subject of the noun clause.)

WRONG: She *laid* there for several hours.

RIGHT: She *lay* there for several hours. (*Laid* is the past of *lay,* meaning to put or place; *lay* in the above sentence is the past of *lie,* meaning to rest or remain.)

WRONG: He filed a motion to try *and* force the attorneys to answer the question. (It should be to try *to* force.)

Do not say *mighta* been for *might have* been; *sorta* for *sort of; kinda* for *kind of; becuz* for *because; irregardless* for *regardless.* (There is no such word as *irregardless.*) RIGHT: *Regardless* of what you say, I do not believe you.

RIGHT: *Those data* should be withheld. (*Data* is plural.) *Exquisite* is accented on the first syllable, not on the second.

Say Feb ru ary, not Feb u ary.

Don't say *couldn't hardly.* There are two negatives there. Say *could hardly.* Don't say *couldn't do nothing.* Say *could do nothing* or *couldn't do anything.*

If a sentence begins with *there is* or *there are,* the verb must agree in number with the noun that follows.

WRONG: There *is* excellent reasons for what you said.

RIGHT: There *are* excellent *reasons* for what you said.

WRONG: On the aisle *was* a lady, a man and a baby.

RIGHT: On the aisle *were a lady, a man* and *a baby.*

WRONG: Firecrackers going off near a *pet* can damage *their* ears.

RIGHT: Firecrackers going off near a *pet* can damage *its/his/ her* ears. (*Pet* is singular, so the antecedent and pronoun must agree in number. *Their* is plural.)


## SHALL AND WILL, SHOULD AND WOULD

When one speaks, it doesn't seem so important to distinguish between these words, but perhaps in writing the distinction should be known and used. To express simple futurity and mere expectation, use *shall* with the first person singular and plural. Use *will* with the second and third person.

I shall play.                      We shall play.
You will play.                     You will play.
He will play.                      They will play.

To show emphatic assurance or resolve, use *will* in the first person and *shall* with the second and third person.

I *will* go.                       We *will* go.
You *shall* do as I say.           You *shall* not go.
He *shall* do it.                  They *shall* not go.

*Should* is like *shall; would* is like *will.*
*None, either, neither, each, no one, nobody, everyone,* and some other words are singular.
WRONG: *Each one* did *their* work well.
RIGHT: *Each one* did *his* work well.
WRONG: *Everyone* of the girls *are* capable.
RIGHT: *Everyone* of the girls *is* capable.
*This* and *that,* if they modify *sort* or *kind,* are singular even though the noun following may be plural.
WRONG: He didn't write *those sort* of letters.
RIGHT: He didn't write *that sort* of letters.
Do not use *don't* with *he, she* or *it.*
WRONG: *He/she/it don't* look happy about the matter. (The verb should be *does*n't.)
Sometimes collective nouns are singular, sometimes plural, depending upon the meaning intended.
RIGHT: The crowd *was* unruly.
RIGHT: The crowd *do* not agree on the issues.
Someone is singular. WRONG: Loving *someone* often includes holding *them* in an idealized position. (Instead of using *them,* one should use *him* or *her* to agree in number with *someone.*)
Nouns and pronouns have GENDER. The genders are masculine (boy, he, etc.), feminine (girl, she, etc.) and neuter (book, kindness, it, etc.)

# More Correct Usage,
# More Faulty Diction

Do not say *ain't*. It is not correct. Say *isn't* or *is not,* or *aren't* or *are not*.

Do not use *awful* as an adverb meaning *very*.

WRONG: He does *awful good*.

RIGHT: He does *very well*.

Do not pronounce *realty* as if it has three syllables. The word is *real ty,* not *real i ty*.

*Between* is used when speaking of two things or persons. *Among* is used when speaking of more than two.

RIGHT: Divide it *between* the two children.

RIGHT: Divide it *among* all of the children.

Do not say, "I could care less about what she thinks."

RIGHT: I couldn't care less about what she thinks.

WRONG: I *use* to say it had no tail.

RIGHT: I *used* to say it had no tail.

WRONG: *Like* I say, I do not like him.

RIGHT: *As* I say, I do not like him. (*Like* is a verb or preposition. *As* is a conjunction.)

Do not say *flustrated* when you mean *frustrated*.

WRONG: I don't smoke *nor* drink.

31

RIGHT: I *neither* smoke *nor* drink; I *don't* smoke *or* drink.

WRONG: The new hotel will be different *than* its predecessor.

RIGHT: The new hotel will be different *from* its predecessor.

Most vowels (a, e, i, o, u) must be preceded by *an*, not *a*. (An apple, an egg, an Indian, an orange, etc.) Some other words beginning with silent letters (such as *honest*) are preceded by *an*.

A verb does not agree with a noun that intervenes between it and the subject.

RIGHT: *Much* of the contents *was* not insured.

WRONG: If a *student* is coming to school, we don't expect *them* to come whenever *they* please.

RIGHT: If a *student* is coming to school, we don't expect *him/her* to come whenever *he/she* pleases. (Agreement of pronoun with its antecedent.)

RIGHT: The *articles were* insured.

RIGHT: *Neither* John nor I *was* insured.

RIGHT: The *size* of the *shoes varies*.

WRONG: The *size* of the shoes *vary*.

WRONG: The *use* of stimulants *are* a menace.

RIGHT: The *use* of stimulants *is* a menace. (Agreement of subject and verb.)

WRONG: The *prices* of grain *changes* each year.

RIGHT: The *prices* of grain *change* every year.

The number of the verb is not changed by the addition to the subject of words beginning with *with, as well as, together with*, etc. RIGHT: The *captain*, as well as other officers, *has* recommended the change. (Not *have*.) A singular subject joined with the words *nor* or *or* takes a singular verb. RIGHT: *Either* the *first* or *second* of the girls in the line *wears* a blue flower. A verb must agree with the *subject*, not with the predicate word (after the linking verb).

WRONG: The worst *thing* in the play *were* the musicians.

RIGHT: The worst *thing* in the play *was* the musicians.

RIGHT: The *musicians were* the worst thing in the play.

*Fine* is an adjective, not an adverb. Do not say *He does fine*. Say *well*. *Good* is an adjective, not an adverb.

*Etc.* is an abbreviation which means *and other things.* Do not use *and etc.* Do not write *ect.* for *etc.*

Some grammarians do not use *gotten* as the past participle of got, but many do. Some use *got.*

*Had of* is not used. RIGHT: I thought I *had heard* about it.
WRONG: I wish I *had of* known about that.
RIGHT: I wish I *had known* about that.

*Had ought* is not used. WRONG: He *had ought* to have known better.
RIGHT: He *ought to have known* better.
RIGHT: He *should have known* better.

Do not use *if* for *whether.* I'm not sure *whether* (not *if*) it will be done tomorrow.

Do not say *kind of:* She was *kind of* stout. RIGHT: She was *somewhat/rather* stout.
WRONG: He *kind of* thought I was going.
RIGHT: He *rather* thought I was going.

If one uses *kind of* before a noun, do not insert *a* before the noun. WRONG: I don't care for that *kind of a* man.
RIGHT: I don't care for that *kind of* man.

In writing, one should use *many* or *much,* not *lots of.*

One should say *might have,* not *might of:* He *might have* gone.

In writing do not use *most* for *almost.* WRONG: *Most* of them went. RIGHT: *Almost* all of them went.

*Neither* is used with *nor; either* is used with *or.*
RIGHT: *Neither* Henry *nor* John was caught.
RIGHT: He was *neither* an artist *nor* a sculptor.

Do not use *nowheres.*

In writing, say *telephone,* not *phone.*

Do not use *providing* for *provided.* WRONG: He will win, *providing* he is a Democrat. RIGHT: He will win *provided* he is a Democrat.

*Quite a few* is not good usage. Say *several, many.*

One *raises* a window or animals, but *rears* children.

*Real* is not an adverb. WRONG: She was *real* pretty. Use *very* or *really*.

*Scarcely* is a negative. WRONG: He couldn*'t scarcely* see. RIGHT: He *could scarcely* see.

*Some* is not an adverb. WRONG: He was *some* better today. Say *somewhat*.

Do not say *superior than*. Say *superior to*.

*Sure* is not an adverb. WRONG: I *sure* hope that you are going. RIGHT: I *surely* hope that you are going.

*Tend* is a verb. One *tends* the store, not *tends to* the store. Jon will *attend to* your needs is correct.

*Them* is an object pronoun, not an adjective. One cannot say I saw *them* children. *Those* children is correct.

Do not use *those kind, those sort*. One should say *this kind, that sort, these kinds, those sorts*.

Do not use *way* for *away*. WRONG: He lived *way* down the street. RIGHT: He lived *away* down the street.

*Ways* is not to be used when referring to distance. A *little way*, not *ways*.

Do not use *which* when referring to people. Use *who* or *that*. WRONG: The boys *which* were in my class were my friends. *Which* or *that* can refer to animals or things.

Do not say *would of*. Say *would have*. He *would have* gone.

Do not say *you was*. Use *were*, both in singular and plural.

*Yourself, myself*, etc., are reflexive pronouns. Do not say *yourself and friend* are invited. Say *you* and friend are invited.

# Spelling

If a word ends in silent *e,* usually drop the *e* before a suffix such as *ing* which begins in a vowel. EXAMPLES: argue, arguing; write, writing; use, using; judge, judging. Exceptions are: dyeing, agreeing. After *c* or *g,* and before a suffix beginning with *a* or *o,* the *e* is retained. EXAMPLES: noticeable, peaceable, serviceable, courageous. (Use your dictionary when in doubt.)

Write: *i* before *e,* except after *c,* or when sounded as *a* as in neighbor and weigh. EXAMPLES: niece, grief; but receive, deceive, ceiling, veil, freight. EXCEPTION: ancient.

Words of one syllable and words accented on the last syllable and ending in a consonant preceded by a single vowel, double the consonant before a suffix beginning with a vowel. EXAMPLES: plan, planned; get, getting; hot, hottest; begin, beginning; repel, repellent. Sometimes *qu* sounds like *w:* quitting, squatter, etc.

Most nouns add *s* or *es* to form the plural. Some, as in leaf, leaves, knife, knives, change *f* to *v* and add *es,* because it sounds better.

If a noun which ends in *y* and is preceded by a consonant is made plural, change *y* to *i* and add *es.* EXAMPLES: lady, ladies; sky, skies, etc. Other nouns which end in *y* form the plural by adding *s.* EXAMPLES: boy, boys; day, days; but donkey, donkeys.

Sometimes it helps one to spell correctly if one thinks of a related word; prepare, prepar*a*tion. This is not always a help, however: four, forty; nine, ninth; please, pleasant, etc.

A few nouns which are different are: ox, oxen; man, men; child, children; sheep, sheep; deer, deer.

Words from foreign languages often keep the foreign plural: index, indices; datum, data; thesis, theses; stratum, strata; Mr., Messrs.; Mrs., Mmes. (Mesdames.)

Compound nouns usually form the plural by adding *s* or *es* to the principal word: sons-in-law, brothers-in-law, passers-by, attorneys-at-law.

New-coined words are usually hyphenated. Old words are often written together: self-evident; bedroom; un-American; unwise. (Consult a dictionary to be sure of the spelling.)

Pronounce words correctly. Notice their syllables. Say ath let ic, not ath a let ic; govern ment, not gov er ment; com par a ble (accent on the first syllable), not com par′ a ble; de fense′, not de′ fense; height, not heighth.

Know the difference between words that sound alike or almost alike: to, too, two; lose, loose; your, you're; their, there, they're; whose, who's (who is); already, all ready; fourth, forth; hear, here; principal, principle; stationery, stationary; sight, cite; formerly, formally; isle, aisle; complement, compliment; caret, carat, carrot; all together, altogether; all ready, already; dining, dinning; diary, dairy; peace, piece; quite, quiet; its, it's; respectfully, respectively, etc.

Watch troublesome words: separate, misspell, embarrass, grammar, etc. Do not spell *all right* incorrectly. There is no such word as *alright*.

A prefix changes the meaning of a root word. *Dis, un, mis* added to the roots become disappear, unwise, misspell.

A suffix is added to the end of a root word. Examples: *ly, ness, able:* generally, goodness, lovable, changeable (after *c* or *g* the final *e* is usually kept). If the root word ends in *y,* change the final *y* to *i* before adding the suffix: happy, happiness; busy, busily.

# Index